INGLIS LECTURES
IN SECONDARY EDUCATION

THE ROLE OF THE FEDERAL
GOVERNMENT IN EDUCATION

LONDON : GEOFFREY CUMBERLEGE
OXFORD UNIVERSITY PRESS

The Inglis Lecture, 1945

The Role of the Federal Government in Education

BY

GEORGE F. ZOOK

President, American Council on Education
Washington, D. C.

CAMBRIDGE
HARVARD UNIVERSITY PRESS

1945

PRINTED AT THE HARVARD UNIVERSITY PRINTING OFFICE
CAMBRIDGE, MASSACHUSETTS, U. S. A.

THE
INGLIS LECTURESHIP

To honor the memory of Alexander Inglis, 1879–1924, his friends and colleagues gave to the Graduate School of Education, Harvard Unversity, a fund for the maintenance of a Lectureship in Secondary Education. To the study of problems in this field Professor Inglis devoted his professional career, leaving as a precious heritage to his co-workers the example of his industry, intellectual integrity, human sympathy, and social vision. It is the purpose of the Lectureship to perpetuate the spirit of his labors and contribute to the solution of problems in the field of his interest. The lectures on this foundation are published annually by the School.

THE ROLE OF THE FEDERAL GOVERNMENT IN EDUCATION

INTRODUCTION

IT is an interesting fact that people seldom, if ever, appreciate the extent and implications of social changes in which they themselves are participants. The length and breadth and depth of what is happening all around us only the discerning historian, writing years later, will be able fully to expound. I know of no social field in which these observations are more true than they are in education.

Yet it is our business as social scientists to discern here and now so far as possible the meaning of changes in the physical world — farming, industry, and transportation — to recognize what is happening to our mode of living — and to appreciate the trend of popular thought. As educators it is our function to make those changes in educational content, organization, support, and methods of instruction called for by our time. We are in duty bound to be creators, not creatures of circumstance.

The role of the federal government in education is one of the important national problems which confront us today. It behooves us as educators, therefore, to acquaint ourselves with its many complexities and ramifications and to exercise such leadership as we can in its consideration and solution. Otherwise we may some day wake up to find, at the end of our generation, as the result of patchwork and piecemeal legislation, a distorted and disjointed national policy in education which represents neither the considered judgment of educational leaders nor the needs of our country. It is my intention therefore in this address to discuss the role of the federal government in education with the hope that such a statement may contribute somewhat to broaden and intensify national consideration of this subject, and with the further hope that all these discussions may some day in the early future result in the adoption of a national policy in education such as we have recently witnessed in Great Britain. It should be clear of course that I am expressing my own personal views and not those of the organization with which I am connected.

I am fully aware of the fact that the subject of this address has received attention from the inception of our federal government; that it took on new significance with the passage of the Morrill Act in 1862; and that during the past generation it has been warmly and widely debated as one of our most important public issues. Two great national commissions appointed by Presidents Herbert Hoover and Franklin D. Roosevelt reported their findings in 1931 and 1938 respectively. The American Youth Commission, composed largely of outstanding laymen, added its recommendations on the subject in *Youth and the Future*, published in 1942. Many other factual reports and pronouncements from other bodies have been forthcoming in recent years, including one just off the press, *Federal-State Relations in Education*, representing the combined opinion of the Educational Policies Commission of the National Education Association and the American Association of School Administrators, and the Problems and Policies Committee of the American Council on Education.

All of these pronouncements are in substantial agreement and it would seem therefore that it is both unnecessary and a bit presumptuous for any one individual to assume that much can be added to the evidence and opinion on this subject which has accumulated, especially during the past fifteen years. It so happens that I have had a modest part, as a participant in many of the more important efforts in this field, where of course it was necessary to merge personal opinions with those of one's associates. Therefore the opportunity graciously extended to me to speak for myself alone on this important subject was a tempting one which I could not resist.

Moreover, with all the study of the problem which has gone on and with all the furore of public debate which arises from time to time with respect to it, I am sure that you will agree with me that we are no nearer a decision on the role of the federal government in education than we were two decades ago. Indeed first the impetus of the depression and then of the present war have served both to emphasize the importance of the problem and to complicate it still further. It is perhaps permissible therefore — indeed I am convinced that it is the deep responsibility — of each individual who is concerned with the preservation and development of our democratic form of government to contribute as best he can to the discussion of this important matter until we arrive at some more satisfactory solution of the problem. I do not assume that in the nature of the problem we can arrive at any final solution but it is important that we recognize and repair any mistakes we have made and that after mature consideration we choose more definitely the general direction which the national policy should follow.

The National Interest in Education

Although education is not mentioned among the powers delegated in the Constitution to the federal government it should by no means be concluded that the founding fathers regarded education as of little or no importance in the national life. As a matter of fact we know that the exact opposite was true. Several of the participants in the Constitutional Convention, either prior to or following the convention, including Washington, Madison, Franklin, and Hamilton, testified to the basic importance which they attached to education in the successful practice of representative government and to the welfare of the nation as a whole.

Later, when Jacksonian democracy began to supplant or supplement the constitutional theory of representative government, there arose in Massachusetts a mighty prophet in the person of Horace Mann to point out the increasing necessity of widespread education in the successful practice of democratic government at all levels, national, state, and local.

Then, having triumphed over the tragedy of the Civil War, we entered into a period of rapid economic and social development which has continued down to the present day and which has given to us an increasing sense of the importance and place of the nation as a whole as against that of the states and the localities in which we live. Rapid transportation brings to our door the products of every region. The news of each section of the country and the world is flashed instantaneously to our homes. Even in wartime, both for business and pleasure, we crowd the facilities for rapid transportation to capacity. In other words, under modern conditions our standard of living, our contacts in the economic realm, our intellectual life, indeed most of our social advantages, we owe increasingly to the nation as a whole.

Into every fiber of this new and constantly developing pattern of our national life education enters, and according to its quality and effectiveness determines the progress which the nation attains. The story of the agricultural development of this country during the past seventy-five years is directly related to agricultural research and education. Modern roads, bridges, railroads, and aviation would be impossible without engineers. Where would we be in the use of rubber, petroleum, and aluminum without the transforming genius of the chemists? What will people do with their increasing leisure unless they fall back on the reading interests stirred in them in the classroom or the wider school of adult life? We know now better than ever before how necessary is popular intelligence if we expect to have successful popular government.

From these scanty and very familiar examples in our economic and social life, which could of course be multiplied indefinitely, one may reaffirm a truth almost universally recognized but from which we do not always deduce the logical conclusion, that not only is education basic to the life of the nation as a whole but that it is therefore desirable for the nation to express its interest and concern with respect to education in any manner which is appropriate in our form of government.

CONSTITUTIONAL CONTROLS OF EDUCATION

In the fundamental law of the land education is not included in the powers to be exercised by the federal government and clearly was intended therefore to be among those numerous powers "which are reserved to the states respectively or to the people." The Supreme Court has upheld this principle upon numerous occasions, as for example on one occasion, in the following words:

> The education of the people in schools maintained by state taxation is a matter belonging to the respective states, and any interference on the part of federal authority with the management of such schools cannot be justified except in the case of a clear and unmistakable disregard of rights secured by the supreme law of the land.

Moreover I doubt whether any principle is more deeply instilled in the minds and hearts of the American people than their conviction that education in this country should be under the control of the states and localities or such private schools as are regularly authorized by the states to undertake such instruction.

Experience has demonstrated amply, however, that in the exercise of the powers delegated to it by the Constitution the federal government inevitably affects the powers which are reserved to the states — and no doubt the opposite is true. For example, the Congress has the "power to . . . provide for the common defence . . . to raise and support Armies . . . and to provide and maintain a Navy." Under this authority the federal government has set up the military and naval academies at West Point and Annapolis and the Coast Guard academy at New London, Connecticut. They prescribe their own admission requirements and curricula. In war, the federal government removes students from any school and college as it deems necessary and uses educational buildings and facilities as it sees fit.

And now further "to provide for the common defence" there is before the Congress bills which require in peacetime every physically fit young man to undergo a year of compulsory military training. One could easily imagine that in the name of national defence the federal government might go still further and, for example, require and support even in peacetime a program of physical training for young persons of high school age. During the past few years we have had a taste of the extent of the federal government's interference with the normal processes of education in war time. Before we are through with it we may have in peacetime innumerable and undreamed of interferences with and modifications of the educational situation by the federal government, all in carrying out its constitutional duty of providing for the common defence.

Or, let us take another interesting situation, where the federal government has exercised tremendous authority with respect to the conduct of education. The Fourteenth Amendment declares that

no State shall make or enforce any law which shall abridge the privileges or immunities of citizens of the United States; nor shall any State deprive any person of life, liberty, or property, without due process of law; *nor deny to any person within its jurisdiction the equal protection of the laws.* (Italics mine.)

Two cases involving this amendment were appealed to the United States Supreme Court from Maryland and Missouri where Negroes were denied admission to curricula offered in the respective state universities to white students but not offered in other state institutions for Negroes within the state.

While the circumstances in the two cases were somewhat different, the Supreme Court held that "if a state furnishes higher education to white residents, it is bound to furnish substantially equal advantages to Negro residents, though not necessarily in the same schools." One can easily imagine the deep reverberations of these recent decisions in the southern and border states, which have traditionally established separate school and college facilities for the two races, but which thus far have neither felt able nor in their opinion has it been necessary to establish duplicate facilities for the two races in all areas of higher education.

Obviously these decisions also have implications in the field of elementary and secondary education which are clear and unmistakable, particularly when taken in connection with the so-called Norfolk Case in which the United States Circuit Court of Appeals ruled that different salary schedules for Negro and white teachers, with identical qualifications and similar duties, were in violation of the "due process" and "equal protection" provisions of the Fourteenth Amendment to the Federal Constitution. At the present time each of the southern and border states is deeply concerned as to what measures it can take to meet such a tremendous interference with its educational system on the part of the federal government under the authority of the Fourteenth Amendment.

Interpretations of the Fourteenth Amendment by the Supreme Court have also affected the powers of the states to control education in other ways. There is, for example, the so-called Oregon Case. In 1922 the State of Oregon passed a law requiring all children from the age of eight to sixteen years to attend public schools. The law was contested by a group of Roman Catholic sisters and a private military academy and was referred to the United States Supreme Court, which held that in exercising its jurisdiction over education within its borders the State of Oregon had violated the rights of individuals as guaranteed under the Fourteenth Amendment to the Constitution. The decision was a momentous one from the point of view of individuals and of private schools.

> The fundamental theory of liberty [so the Court declared], upon which all governments of this Union repose excludes any general power of the State to standardize its children by forcing them to accept instruction from public teachers only. The child is not the mere creature of the State; those who nurture him and direct his destiny have the right, coupled with the high duty, to recognize and prepare him for additional obligations.

This decision was of course another assertion of federal as against state authority, involving an important limitation of the power of the states to regulate education. It was indeed an important supplement to the famous Dartmouth College Case, which denied the right of the state to interfere with rights and privileges conferred on colleges by the colonial charters.

Closely related to the Oregon Case was the decision in the Nebraska Case and by implication in a number of other states, which responding to popular hysteria relative to the teaching of German during and following World War I passed acts forbidding the teaching of foreign languages to students who had not finished the eighth grade in private, parochial, or public schools. The Nebraska law, as it applied to private and parochial schools, was carried to the Supreme Court, where it was held that the right of the teacher — in this case a modern language teacher — "to teach and the right of parents to engage him to instruct their children . . . are within the liberty of the (Fourteenth) Amendment." The law was therefore pronounced as "arbitrary and without reasonable relation to any end within the competency of the state."

With respect to this decision, Newton Edwards of the University of Chicago declared a few years ago:

> The significance of this case will be more fully appreciated

when it is recalled that ten other states had in force substantially the same kind of legislation as had Nebraska, and that in two other states the Supreme Court had upheld the constitutionality of such legislation. In a single decision, therefore, the Supreme Court of the United States reversed an important educational policy of approximately one-fourth of the States of the Union.

So much for the exercise of federal control over education growing out of the application of the Fourteenth Amendment to the Constitution. Let us consider for a moment the possible implications, especially for privately supported education, of the application of the federal tax laws also based on Constitutional authority. The utilization of the present exemption of 15 per cent of one's income for charitable and educational gifts in the income tax law is wholly a matter of Congressional provision and if withdrawn or severely curtailed would seriously affect the stability and future of privately controlled schools and colleges. Likewise, if a percentage ceiling upon philanthropic bequests under the estate tax law should be adopted by Congress, as has been recently proposed by the Treasury Department, it would doubtless have a similar depressing effect upon the development of these educational institutions and even to a considerable extent on publicly controlled schools and colleges which now, more frequently than formerly, receive considerable amounts in private benefactions.

May I cite still another example of possible federal interference with education. We have all come to believe in a broad program of social security. In the presidential campaign a few months ago the two major parties vied with one another in calling for its extension to groups of employees not now included in the system, such as those connected with charitable and educational institutions. School and college teachers have long been seeking adequate provisions for retirement for disability or old age. A number of states have set up more or less adequate provisions for individuals employed in public schools and colleges. Many privately controlled and some publicly controlled colleges have set up retirement systems of their own or in coöperation with the Teachers Insurance and Annuity Association.

Let us suppose now that the Congress enacts a law extending the old age and survivors insurance provisions of the Social Security Act to the teachers and other employees in schools and colleges. Quite apart from what would amount to an indirect subsidy by the federal government to all types of schools and colleges would be ultimately the federal requirement of a 3 per cent contribution by the schools and colleges in order to match a similar contribution from their employees. I do not cite this example in order to question the action, because I believe firmly in the extension of the social security system, but it is another example of federal interference with the conduct of education in order to carry out a wider program of "general welfare."

Numerous other instances of federal interference with the control of education through powers granted to it in the Constitution could easily be cited. These are sufficient, however, I am sure, to indicate the length and breadth of these powers as they are being exercised through legislation and court interpretations. It is clear, in the first place, that through the application of the Constitution, the federal government is protecting some of the most deeply rooted liberties of individuals against the hasty and arbitrary actions of the states. The hopes of the Negro for equal educational opportunities in the South are deeply dependent on the Fourteenth Amendment, as are also the rights and privileges of private schools and the rights of individuals to send their children to such schools. Equally important are the extensive controls over education which may be exercised by the federal government at all levels through the power and obligation of the federal government to provide for the common defense and in the exercise of its taxing powers. Furthermore we may probably look forward to extensions of these controls in the future in directions not now suspected.

"General Welfare" and Education

There is still another provision of the federal Constitution to which I now wish to call your attention. Among the powers assigned to the Congress is one to "provide for the . . . general welfare of the United States." The Supreme Court has never given us a comprehensive interpretation of what is meant by the "general welfare" clause of the Constitution and the powers which the federal government, under this authority, may and should exercise. The other powers delegated to the Congress in this section — defense, patents, money, naturalization, taxes, war, courts, etc. — are all very specific. "General welfare" alone seems indefinite and open to wide interpretation.

We shall therefore have to await the long succession of laws and court decisions, many of which consciously or unconsciously will be based upon this broad provision in the Constitution. Federal legislation has already been enacted on such exceedingly important matters as housing, social security, reclamation, reforestation, the construction of dams, relief, roads, public health, and the support of education.

Thus the power of providing for the general welfare

has taken on increasingly definite meaning. In the development of this program the Congress has not hesitated to make large appropriations of money to be expended in the states to implement "general welfare" functions that are commonly thought of as state and local functions.

Presumably therefore the federal government offers its financial assistance in many instances in order that a state and local function may thereby be carried on more effectively. Theoretically there may be no transfer of authority implied in the process but, as everyone knows, the federal government, through successive appropriation measures, may place increasing restrictions on the use of federal funds and thus transfer a corresponding amount of authority to a federal agency. For obvious reasons there have been few cases in court which called such federal action into question, and, in the small number of cases which have occurred, federal legislative provisions have been upheld on the theory that the state is free to accept or reject the money if it does not like the accompanying restrictions on the federal grants.

Not only the Constitution but, as I have stated, earlier economic and social developments within the country justify a proper concern on the part of the federal government with the general welfare. A rather high proportion of the people born in each state of the Union sooner or later migrate to other states, temporarily or permanently. Sometimes, as in the case of the Negro migration from the southern states to northern cities during the past two decades, or as in the mass migration from rural areas to defense plant centers during the present war, the movement of population is extensive. Certainly the quality of citizenship in which education or the lack of it plays an important part is a matter of deep concern, not only to the states and the localities within those states to which the migrants go, but also to the nation as a whole.

Even more pertinent in our thinking at the present time is the fact that approximately 4,500,000 men have been rejected by draft boards for military service since the passage of the Selective Service Act on account of educational, mental, or physical deficiencies. It is generally conceded that a substantial proportion of these deficiencies might have been remedied through the processes of education. Certainly it would be in the interests of the country's "general welfare," if not for its "common defence," that the federal government should take steps to eliminate as much of this disgraceful condition as possible.

Or let us consider for a moment another situation the importance of which we have been made aware of, both in peace and war. Until a generation ago we were largely a nation of farmers and commercial people. Although certain industries had been protected from foreign competition by tariffs we had comparatively few skilled craftsmen as compared to certain foreign countries. This seemed likely to retard our industrial development indefinitely and to make it impossible to meet foreign competition. The realization of this situation was one of the direct causes for the interest in and final passage of the Smith-Hughes Vocational Act. Under the stimulus of this act, and with the aid of federal funds, we have made great progress toward the repairing of this deficiency. On the solid foundation already laid it was possible to expand the training program during the present war quickly and effectively. There has always been question concerning certain provisions of this act, but who can doubt that it has been well worth while for the federal government to have expended many millions of dollars to provide adequately for this aspect of the country's "defence" and "general welfare."

Finally, in this discussion of education as an aspect of the general welfare I wish to call attention to a very practical situation the significance of which has never been generally appreciated. In February 1913, action was completed on the Sixteenth Amendment to the Constitution, which reads as follows:

> The Congress shall have power to lay and collect taxes on income, from whatever sources derived, without apportionment among the several states and without regard to any census or enumeration.

The right of the federal government to levy income taxes is by this amendment explicit and clear. The amendment did not, of course, prevent the states also from collecting income taxes, and at the present time nearly three-fourths of them do so. But in effect the states, through the Sixteenth Amendment, surrendered to the federal government what has turned out to be one of the most fruitful sources of income. In the fiscal year ending June 30, 1940, thirty-one states collected $205,979,000 in income taxes as against $982,017,000 collected by the federal government. In 1944 thirty-three states collected from the same source $335,870,000, as against the federal government's $18,262,000,000. In other words in the year before the effects of the war became evident, the federal government was already collecting nearly five times as much in income taxes as the states. At the height of the war the federal government collected more than fifty times the amount obtained by the states from this tax source.

This tremendous transfer of taxing power to the federal government could not help but have exceedingly important implications. To be sure the Congress had prior to the passage of this amendment made a number of appropriations to the states which might fall under the heading of "general welfare," but they were insignificant in amount as compared to what came after. It is no accident that it was after the passage of the Sixteenth Amendment that Congress entered into or expanded such large general welfare programs as vocational education, agricultural research, extension in agriculture and home economics, roads, housing, child welfare, health, and social security. In other words, it was now practical for the federal government to finance great general welfare enterprises, including education, for the benefit of the people in all the states of the Union which otherwise would have progressed in an uncoördinated manner only in the more wealthy states.

As I have pointed out before, some of these "general welfare" enterprises, notably education, are activities in which the federal government has properly a deep concern, but the control of these enterprises was originally intended to be "reserved to the States . . . or to the people." Moreover the people generally seem to be deeply convinced of the desirability of state, local, and institutional control of education and they have set up their schools and colleges accordingly. It is to the interest of the federal government to make such a function as education more effective through financial assistance but not to enter into competition with the states and localities for the control of education. Thus the states and the federal government are inevitably in partnership on many areas of "general welfare," including education. This conception is well stated in an exhaustive report submitted to the United States Treasury Department several years ago by a committee composed of Harold M. Groves, Luther H. Gulick, and

Mabel Newcomer, entitled *Federal, State and Local Government Fiscal Relations.* The first sentence in this exhaustive study declares that

Coordination and cooperation rather than subordination and coercion is the answer to inter-governmental fiscal problems in the United States.

Later, the report continues,

The superior strategic position of the Federal Government in the control of large-scale business, is the stabilization of employment and production, and in the maximumization of national income has justified aggressive Federal leadership and the expansion of Federal activities in recent years. But this expansion need not be at the expense of the states and the municipalities. The major consideration is how best the states may participate in this expansion, and how best they may facilitate it rather than retard it. The states still continue to retain large responsibility for many governmental services close to the welfare of the citizen. The Federal Government has a vital interest in maintaining and strengthening both state and local governments. . . . Coordination has become a major problem in the operation of the Federal Government.

The same idea was expressed exceedingly well in the report of the National Advisory Committee on Education in 1931 as follows

Obviously no one type of government should attempt to parallel all the responsibilities and all the functions of the others. Nor should we foster the disposition to locate all responsibility and commensurate authority in education upon any single governmental level. Together they should supplement, complement, and reinforce each other in the achievement of the common national purpose.

Our civilization seems to call for neither complete local decentralization, where we began, nor for the exercise of complete state power, which is the existing legal theory, nor for an increasing federal management and control, toward which policy we have been recently tending.

Experience seems to indicate that we require a balanced distribution of educational obligations and functions on all governmental levels.

The federal government is therefore often essential to the carrying out of a function in the most effective manner. It is inconceivable, for example, that our great system of highways could have been developed without the leadership and financial support of the federal government. It would have been a national misfortune if the federal government had not had both the vision and the courage to take a leading part in their development. Do you suppose that some day, in the not distant future, we may look back similarly on a splendid system of hospitals, airways, libraries, and school buildings with something of the same pride, because the federal government has helped to provide the financial resources with which to construct them?

We should not therefore think of the federal government as a thing apart but as an instrumentality to be used for such purposes as may seem desirable. It belongs to us just as truly as our state and local governments. It can be and is operated as democratically and as effectively as our state and local governments. Indeed one often hears that local governments, which presumably are closer to the people than either the state or federal governments, are frequently least responsive to the public will and least efficient in the conduct of public affairs. From this we may well conclude that we should operate many of our public interests, including education, through the several levels of government by assigning to each the role in which it respectively can be most effective. On this score the use of the federal government to attain educational objectives is certainly entitled to consideration and we ought to have no hesitation in using it wherever it can accomplish results which may not reasonably be expected of states, localities, and privately controlled schools and colleges through their own limited and uncoördinated resources.

Unequal Opportunity for Education in the States

It is of course generally agreed that not only the control but the financial support of public education rests primarily upon the states and localities. Were it possible for the several states to support education on anything like an equivalent basis or even upon a defensible minimum basis, the issue of federal aid to education, with all of its attendant problems, would never be raised except perhaps where a national emergency was involved.

Unhappily this is not the case and instead of what would appear to be the natural birthright of every child in America for something like an equal opportunity for education we have in fact a shocking inequality of educational opportunity which, as I have said before, is properly not only the concern of the respective states and localities but of the nation as a whole.

So much fine work has been accomplished in recent years in uncovering and setting forth the evidence in this situation as to make it impossible and quite unnecessary for me to review the evidence in detail. Suffice it for me to cite very briefly some of the major considerations.

In the first place let it be realized that for some time the birth rate in the rural areas has been considerably higher than it has been in urban centers. There are also considerable disparities in this regard between and among the several major sections of the country. As a result of this situation the number of children of school age to be supported in school by each 1,000 in the adult population is much greater in some states than it is in others. For example in the state of South Carolina there are slightly more than twice as many children of school age (5–17 years) per 1,000 adults as there are in California.

This situation alone might easily account for considerable inequalities in educational opportunity between and among the various states. But there are others of equal or greater significance. I refer to the well-known fact that the average per capita income — the basis on which schools and colleges as well as other social enterprises must be supported — also varies greatly from one state to another, depending in general upon the degree to which the people of a state pursue agriculture, industry, mining, or commerce for a livelihood. Thus the inhabitants of Nevada in 1940 had a per capita income of $960 while in Mississippi the corresponding figure was $195, a spread of almost five times.

By an interesting coincidence which is not at all surprising, the states with the largest educational load per 1,000 population are in general the very states which have the smallest per capita wealth and income with which to support the education of their children. The result is that it is quite impossible for the people of the several states to support their schools and colleges on anything like an equivalent basis, even though most of the poorer states, realizing the basic significance of education in the welfare of the state, have usually made especially valiant efforts to provide educational opportunities comparable to those in the more wealthy states. But it is a hopeless struggle. It simply cannot be done. For example, while the number of children of school age per thousand population in the nation is 226, California with relatively high financial resources has the lightest educational load of the states and must provide schools for only 178 per 1,000 population, while South Carolina, a state which ranks low in economic resources, must provide school facilities for 296 children per 1,000 population.

It should not be surprising therefore that in many states where the educational load is large, where, too, the per capita wealth and income are comparatively low, in spite of unusual effort to meet the situation, educational opportunity and results are and must be under present circumstances comparatively low. For example in the school year 1941–42 New York State paid an average salary of $2,604 to its public school teachers while the corresponding figure in Mississippi was only $559. Similarly the average current expense per pupil in average daily attendance ranged from $168.07 in New York State schools to $31.52 in Mississippi. With respect to the number of days per year attended by each pupil in school, the spread was from 166 days in Wisconsin to 118 days in Mississippi.

I realize that a high level of teachers' salaries, long school years, a high proportion of the school population in school, and even a high rate of literacy may not be relied upon alone to produce good citizens. Nevertheless in such studies as have been made from time to time as to achievement in the various school subjects there is usually a positive correlation between the school achievement of the pupils and such objective factors in the schools as I have just cited, including particularly the amount of financial support which is available.

In the face of these facts I do not see how anyone

who has examined carefully the overwhelming evidence brought to light by numerous researches in recent years can fail to reach the conclusion that federal aid to education in the states graduated according to their needs is both desirable and necessary. Based on data for the year 1939–40 it would take $316,000,000 to lift the level of financial support of every classroom in the United States which is now below the national median up to that level, namely $1,600. To make that figure even more meaningful for this audience may I say that the median level of classroom support in Massachusetts exceeds $2,500 per year. In my opinion we should urge on Congress at once and with all our power the passage of a bill providing at least $500,000,000 per year to the states toward the equalizing of educational opportunities within the respective states, and, as I shall speak of later, to assist needy and talented students to continue their education in school and college. I do not believe any other measure now before Congress except those which are necessary for the defense of the country would contribute more to the general welfare of the country. At the end of the war an equal amount of money should be appropriated annually for a limited number of years to assist states and localities to construct school and library buildings.

FEDERAL CONTROLS AND FEDERAL AID TO EDUCATION

The question at once arises as to what controls if any may properly be included in legislation which the Congress passes in order to provide financial assistance to the states with respect to the support of education. Here one is confronted always with two practical difficulties. The first is the fact that the sponsors of such legislation often have pet ideas which they would like to see accomplished through the federal legislation and which to them it seems almost heresy to question. Secondly the members of Congress often hesitate to hand over money to the states for educational purposes without setting up restrictions upon its expenditure. In other words, it is natural for them to feel that inasmuch as they are making the appropriations they too should have a good deal to say concerning the conditions under which it may be expended. In both cases the educator and the legislator, although they usually protest their deep devotion to the principle of state and local control in education, are likely to weaken in one direction or another when actually confronted with a legislative situation.

Nevertheless with the exceptions of those federal controls of education plainly provided for in the Constitution it seems to me that both the letter of the Constitution and the spirit of the American people clearly agree that the control of education should be reserved to the people, to be exercised through their state and local governments, including the provisions which every state makes for the establishment and conduct of schools and colleges under private control. I believe that it is exceedingly important that we exercise this function through state and local authorities and that every bill passed by Congress in aid of or dealing with education should recognize the prior and I believe constitutional rights of the people to administer their educational enterprises through these levels of government. Liberty in the conduct of education is one of our most priceless possessions, fundamental to the development of American democratic and religious life, and we shall be very unwise if we hand it over, even in exchange for federal funds, to the central government to any greater degree than modern life and the application of constitutional powers plainly require.

From the standpoint of general principles, therefore, it ought to follow that any bill in aid of education in the states should contain no provisions for federal control of the expenditure of these funds except the usual ones for auditing and reporting and those which grow out of the application of the provisions of the Constitution, including particularly the Fourteenth Amendment. In other words, the federal funds should be passed over to the states with no strings attached to them, to be expended in accordance with the respective desires of the several states.

Yet, the extent and variety of federal control already present in existing legislation providing aid for education in the states is by no means inconsiderable, and an examination of bills now before Congress does not lead one to conclude that this tendency is decreasing.

For the most part this control has been of an external nature rather than of an internal type. It has consisted, for example, of choosing certain areas of education such as vocational education and extension education in agriculture and home economics for special assistance to the exclusion of other types of education; or it has consisted of a requirement, as in the Smith-Hughes and the Smith-Lever laws, that the states and localities should match the federal funds on a 50/50 basis, or, as in the vocational act, it has consisted in provisions that the federal funds should be expended only in public schools; or, as in the Smith-Lever act, it consists of broad powers given to the federal authority to accept or reject state plans for the expenditure of both the federal and state funds required in the federal legislation.

In view of the temptation throughout federal legislation dealing with federal aid to education to insert various external controls, it may be appropriate to discuss briefly several of the more usual ones.

The first is the tendency for groups or organizations interested in a particular form of education to promote its wide and rapid extension through special federal appropriations for that purpose. The Morrill acts, the vocational education acts, the rehabilitation acts, and the extension education acts are the best examples to date. The motives of the initiators are commendable, the need is usually pressing, and the regular educational system in the states is often slow to perceive the rising importance of the field; and finally many of the states are unable financially to provide the necessary support even where the need is appreciated. Hence the groups interested in these particular areas of education repair to Washington, full of commendable zeal, to accomplish a great purpose at one stroke through federal legislation. In this process they necessarily, through federal legislation, arbitrarily select their field of interest, for example, to include only the vocations of agriculture, home making, and trades and industries. Or, as in the Second Morrill Act of 1890, the federal money can "be applied only to instruction in agriculture, the mechanic arts, the English language and the various branches of mathematics, physical, natural and economic science, with special reference to their applications in the industries of life," etc.

In view of the very significant contributions to American education which have been made as a result of federal assistance to special fields of education; in view also of the importance which they have been to American national life, including even the defense of our country; and granting the necessity of such steps as temporary measures, I believe that the time has now arrived when we should adopt a comprehensive program of federal aid to education which is large enough for all purposes and which places the responsibility squarely on the states and localities for developing their respective educational programs. The competition for recognition and support between and among the various types of education can then be fought out and decided in the several states of the Union, where such matters should be decided, rather than in Washington where in my opinion they ought not to be decided.

In the early vocational and extension legislation the states, in order to secure the federal subsidies, had to agree to match them with state or local funds on a 50/50 basis. It seems strange now, that at the time the legislation was passed it should not have been realized that the matching funds would be supplied primarily by the localities and that this in turn would mean that the communities which were financially able to do so would match and secure the federal funds, whereas the poorer counties and communities, where the need might really be greater, would be less able to secure the federal funds. This situation has caused much unfavorable comment and practically all studies of the federal aid situation have since condemned matching provisions in no uncertain terms.

However, notwithstanding widespread opinion in agreement with this belief, no one has ever made a serious attempt to amend either the original Smith-Hughes law or the Smith-Lever act so as to eliminate these provisions, which is of course eloquent evidence of the fact that any form of federal control once written into federal legislation is likely to remain indefinitely no matter what the general and professional opinion may be with respect to its desirability. It should be stated, however, that attempts to alleviate this discrimination against the poorer counties and communities have been made through supplementary and more recent legislation.

It is exceedingly difficult to dispose of this issue once and for all, however, for the simple reason that federal grants in connection with such huge enterprises as roads and social security are based on state offsets which drain state funds away from the support of all other state activities, including education, and thus leave the support of education in a relatively unprotected position. For example, Congress last year authorized annual grants to the states of $500,000,000 for the construction of trunk highways in the first three years of the postwar era, provided the several states match it on a 50/50 basis.

This action by Congress may well prove to be a major interference with education by reviving the argument for 50/50 appropriations or some modification of it. At any rate, in the latest pronouncement on Federal-State Relations in Education, made jointly by the Problems and Policies Committee of the American Council on Education and the Educational Policies Commission, one finds the following warning:

As a matter of general policy the required matching of federal funds should be avoided. However, if matching continues to be required in connection with other federal subsidies such as those for roads and old age security, it may be also necessary in the case of education if it is not to be put in an unfavorable position in connection with state budgeting

One interesting suggestion to accomplish this objective is the provision for variable grants to the states in terms of the relative financial ability of the several states. It still seems to me, however, that we would be on much sounder ground to refrain from this form of federal control, particularly as it has been applied to the support of special areas of education, and to endeavor to educate our friends in roads and social security to follow our example.

Still another type of federal control in education has been what may seem to be the natural tendency to confine federal subsidies to the support of public schools only. The Smith-Hughes vocational act does so and the general federal aid bills have usually contained stringent provisions along this line. Nevertheless it should be clear that this too is a form of external federal control which prevents the states from using their own judgments in the expenditure of these funds. By contrast the original Morrill act contained no such provision and therefore the Commonwealth of Massachusetts has for many years seen fit to use the funds arising out of this act for the support of engineering at the Massachusetts Institute of Technology rather than to establish a college of engineering in connection with the state college of agriculture as all other states have done. I am sure you will realize that I am not here attempting to pass on the wisdom of this action, but merely to point out that it is in accordance with American educational tradition and practice that the matter should be determined by state and not by federal action.

The supporters of privately controlled education are equally prone to seek a decision on the use of federal funds for the support of privately controlled education at the federal level rather than the state level. This fact arises out of two situations. In the first place, practically all states, rightly or wrongly, have confined the use of their own funds to the support of public schools and colleges. In most instances therefore private schools and colleges, no matter how much they feel that they are entitled to such support, have been unable to secure it and they see no reason to suppose that there will be any significant change in the attitudes of the states over the long future.

Secondly, recent developments, especially during the depression and the war, have brought a certain realignment of thought on this important matter at the federal level. I refer to the various provisions made by the federal government to aid individuals to attend schools and colleges. Even a brief review of these provisions makes an impressive total. For example, as early as 1918 there was the veterans' rehabilitation act providing for the vocational rehabilitation of soldiers, sailors, and marines entirely at federal expense. Then came the civilian rehabilitation act of 1920 which has been amended from time to time. Under the Act of July 6, 1943, as was pointed out in the recent annual report of the Office of Vocational Rehabilitation, vocational rehabilitation is "available under the federal-state program to all disabled persons who can profit from this service." The law provides for payment to individuals and for their instructional and rehabilitation expenses during the period of training. During the fiscal year ending June 30, 1944, rehabilitation services were rendered to 145,059 men and women.

Then came the student aid program of the National Youth Administration through which students in all types of secondary schools and colleges were enabled to earn a substantial portion of their expenses while attending schools and colleges. In May 1940, for example, 349,248 young people were employed on part-time work programs while attending secondary schools, and 129,144 in universities and colleges, total 478,392. The student aid program began in 1934 and was discontinued in 1943.

The E.S.M.W.T. training program for war industries carried on by the United States Office of Education gave financial assistance to a large number of individuals while they were in training at educational institutions both public and private.

Even the specialized war training programs undertaken by the Army and Navy in a large number of the colleges and universities for men and women in uniform are a form of financial aid to individuals which will be of permanent educational value to the recipients after the end of hostilities.

Finally, there are of course the provisions of the act for the rehabilitation of military personnel disabled in the present war and the better known provisions of the Servicemen's Readjustment Act of 1944, popularly known as the GI bill, under the terms of which war veterans receive $50 per month ($75 per month if there are one or more dependents) to attend the school or college of their choice. Already 14,599 veterans are enrolled in school and college under this act, and it is believed that after the war well over one million veterans will avail themselves of the financial assistance offered to them by the federal government to obtain the advantages of better education for themselves.

Closely related to this situation is the fact that the Servicemen's Readjustment Act also authorizes the payment of the usual tuition and fees charged by the institutions up to $500 for the academic year. Inasmuch as these fees are usually higher in the privately controlled institutions it seems possible and probable that as a group they will collect more money from the federal government for the same services than will be received by the publicly controlled institutions. This situation seems even more certain in the school field where in the vocational schools, for example, in which many thousands of veterans will ultimately be registered, fees are either extremely low or nonexistent as against private schools where the tuition fees pay all or almost all of the cost involved.

The examples of federal financial assistance to individuals to attend school or college begun before and during the war and which in the case of the war veterans is now exceedingly small as compared to what it will be following the close of hostilities are bound to have a profound effect upon the thinking of the public with respect to the form which federal aid to education should take. Already one of the federal aid bills now in Congress would if passed authorize an appropriation of $150,000,000 a year for the purpose of enabling needy persons between the ages of fourteen and twenty inclusive to continue their education in either privately controlled or publicly controlled schools and colleges.

It is not surprising also that among the charges recently given to the Office of Scientific Research and Development by President Roosevelt one finds the following request: "Can an effective program be proposed for discovering and developing scientific talent in American youth so that the continuing future of scientific research in this country may be assured on a level comparable to what has been done during the war? "

It is indeed appropriate that towards the end of the war in Europe, in which science has proved to be so powerful a weapon, consideration should be given to the development of a system for identifying and giving financial aid to youth who show evidence of superior talent in scientific fields to attend any qualified university or college of their choice. So far as I know it is generally agreed that such a plan, within appropriate limits, would be both in the interest of the "common defence" and the "general welfare" of the nation.

To expand a system of aid for needy and talented students extensively, however, so that it in effect settles the issue in Washington as to whether federal funds are to be used in the support of privately as well as publicly controlled institutions, instead of leaving this decision to the states, raises once more, in a different form, one of the most difficult problems which we face. Already, as I have pointed out, there is extensive precedent for allowing the individual so aided to attend either type of institution in the rehabilitation acts, the N.Y.A. student aid program, and the Servicemen's Readjustment Act. Moreover, in one state, New York, there has been for years a state scholarship system in aid of individuals who may attend any approved college or university of their choice. In Massachusetts, however, in 1922 the Attorney General declared that a scholarship system, similar to that obtaining in New York, would in effect constitute financial support of privately controlled institutions of higher education and hence would be in violation of the constitution of the Commonwealth. In Pennsylvania, where a state system of scholarships is being proposed to aid students to attend liberal arts colleges in the state, the state teachers colleges are considerably exercised about the possible effects of such a scholarship system on their future development, or perhaps their very existence.

Therefore, while in my opinion it is entirely appropriate and very desirable for the federal government to support programs of financial assistance to both needy and talented students to attend any school or college of their choice, these programs should not be regarded as a substitute for federal financial aid to the states, to be used by them in whatever manner they see fit for the equalization of educational opportunity. One may conclude from this discussion that a limited portion of the federal appropriations to the states in aid of education should be available for student assistance.

In this connection attention should be called to the fact that recently an advisory committee appointed by the Committee on Education in the House of Representatives, after compiling exhaustive information as to the plight of many colleges resulting from the war, rendered a report recommending among other things that

(a) A non-partisan Commission on Emergency Aid to Higher Educational Institutions be appointed to receive and approve applications for stand-by and other service contracts. . . . That Congress appropriate a sum of 25 million dollars for the fiscal year beginning July 1, 1945, to provide such aid and to pay the costs of administration; (b) If the Congress provides for a program of public works, grants-in-aid be given higher educational institutions for repair and reconstruction or replacement of permanent equipment and repairing or remodeling and construction of buildings, on the same bases as for other public works.

It is apparent at once that the temporary aid through "stand-by and other service contracts" recommended in this report would go largely to privately controlled colleges now in distress and that the grants-in-aid for repairing and constructing buildings would, contrary to the law under which P.W.A. operated before the war, go to privately controlled as well as publicly controlled colleges. Should the Congress accept these recommendations there would, of course, in such action be important implications of federal policy with respect to education over the long future.

I have set forth several of the more important ways — there are others — in which privately controlled schools and colleges have received financial support directly from the federal government during the war and some indications of the possible extent of it after the war. Most, but by no means all of it, has been at the level of higher education. I have no doubt that should another war occur the federal government would again use and support all types of schools and colleges in whatever manner seemed to serve the war needs of the country most effectively. Moreover, I assume that we may learn some permanent lessons as to the defense of the country through the use of schools and colleges in peacetime which it may be appropriate for the federal government to support. Nevertheless I wish to raise frankly the question as to whether the long-time support of privately controlled schools and colleges from public funds, including those supplied by the federal government, should not be fought out at the state level. Unless we stick by this policy we shall inevitably have an increasing amount of federal control of education, brought on in considerable part by those who have protested most loudly against it.

The Federal Government and the Education of Negroes

The situation calling for the most sympathy in the way of external federal control of education has usually been the case of the separate schools for Negroes in the southern and border states. The inequality of their educational opportunities in comparison with those of the whites is too well known to need elaboration. Suffice it to say that, generally speaking, teachers in Negro schools are not so well prepared or paid as are white teachers. School buildings and teaching facilities are generally inferior and high school education is often not available at all. In simple justice, therefore, those who have considered national legislation in aid of education in the states have been strongly tempted to include some provision in the legislation which would guarantee a fair distribution of such federal funds to the Negroes as well as to the whites. Indeed the Second Morrill Act of 1890, which began the practice of distributing funds to the several states in aid of colleges of agriculture and mechanic arts, contained the following provision:

> No money shall be paid out under this act to any state or territory for the support and maintenance of a college where a distinction of race or color is made in the admission of students, but the establishment and maintenance of such colleges separately for white and colored students shall be held to be a compliance with the provisions of this act, if the funds received in such state or territory be equitably divided.

Since that time no other permanent federal legislation in aid of education, notably the vocational education act and the agricultural and home economics extension act, have included provisions for the protection of Negroes, with the result that these services have been organized respectively in the white land-grant colleges and for the most part in aid of white vocational schools.

However, the Federal Security Agency appropriations act for the war production training programs forbids discrimination because of "sex, race or color" and in states with separate schools requires equitable provisions for facilities and training of "like equality."

On the other hand, one of the present bills for federal aid to education before Congress contains the following provision: "States where separate public schools are maintained for separate races," which wish to qualify for the receipt of federal funds in aid of education must, among other things, "provide for a just and equitable apportionment of such funds for the benefit of public schools maintained for minority races, without reduction of the proportion of state and local moneys expended for educational purposes."

As might be expected, the various national commissions which have considered this extremely difficult problem involving a conflict between one's belief in state and local control of education on the one hand, and a pitiful practical situation on the other, have perhaps quite naturally not adopted a consistent attitude on the matter. The National Advisory Committee on Education, which in 1931 submitted the most vigorous and consistent argument in favor of state and local control of education ever set forth in this country, declared that

the policies regarding dependence on local autonomy, and regarding federal grants for education in general to be administered by the states . . . when applied to the Negroes, will in the end result in more lasting benefit to them than would federal action directed toward supplying quickly any special educational facilities for the Negroes under supervision or administration.

From this recommendation the three Negro members of the committee dissented vigorously, maintaining that the country as a whole was morally obligated to the uplift of this section of the population so recently freed from slavery, that the situation affected the life of the entire nation, and finally that a precedent for the equitable distribution of federal funds had been set in the Second Morrill Act, which had worked successfully.

The President's Advisory Committee on Education, which made a very careful study of the educational situation in the several states and of the relation of education to the national economy, recognized in its report in 1938 the need for various types of improvements in the educational situation within the states, as, for example, better prepared teachers, better school buildings, and better state departments of education, which should be accomplished in part through federal funds earmarked for these purposes. It was therefore natural that this committee should take a different point of view with respect to the Negro situation as follows:

> For all states maintaining separate schools for Negroes, the proposed grants should be conditioned upon formulation of joint plans providing an equitable distribution of the federal grants between white and Negro schools, without reduction of the proportion of state and local funds spent for Negro schools.

The American Youth Commission in its report in January 1942 after calling attention to the undesirable situation in the Negro schools and the recent decisions of the Supreme Court against discriminations in educational matters by local or state authorities, which obviously were based on race or color, declared that nondiscrimination between races in educational matters through these decisions "has become a part of the law of the land, marking a step forward which must be implemented by suitable fiscal measures."

Here we have a declaration to the effect that special provisions protecting the interests of the Negro are on an entirely different footing than is true of other federal controls which may be found in a federal aid bill. In other words, the federal government is now committed through the Supreme Court decisions, to which I referred earlier, to bring about equitable opportunities in education within the respective states between white and colored people. It cannot therefore very well refrain from seeing to it that the funds which it makes available to the states in aid of education actually implement a fundamental right guaranteed in the Constitution as interpreted by the Supreme Court.

What further steps may properly be taken by the federal government to implement these decisions may well produce interesting speculations. Senator Langer, for example, when the federal aid bill was before Congress last year, succeeded in securing an amendment to the bill requiring that before a state could become eligible for the receipt of federal funds it must show that there was no discrimination in the distribution of state and local funds for educational purposes on account of race, creed, or color. The move was undoubtedly a legislative ruse to defeat the bill, but it serves to bring out the fact that the federal government is now obligated to see to it that equal opportunities are open to children of the two races within the respective states. What the program of the federal government will be to accomplish this purpose in the years to come will be interesting to observe. Certainly we are not through with the measures which will be taken to this end. Indeed the principle as already observed elsewhere is so far-reaching as to justify and require federal action in a variety of directions not now generally appreciated.

INTERNAL CONTROLS OF EDUCATION

The previous discussion has related primarily to what I have chosen to call external controls of education through federal legislation. Some people have been inclined not to view this form of federal control with much alarm because it was assumed to be relatively unimportant; others have regarded such controls as more or less necessary; still others question them but accept them as being inevitable. I believe you will agree with me, however, that they are of very great importance and that the traditional control of education by state and local authorities may be in the process of being transferred to Washington to a much larger degree than we dreamed of only a decade ago.

It is therefore reassuring to point out the firm stand which is still being taken by educators and laymen alike on what may be called the internal control of education as illustrated by the following declaration in one of the present federal aid bills before Congress:

> No department, agency, officer or employee of the United States shall . . . with respect to . . . any funds . . . made available or expended pursuant to this act . . . direct, supervise, or control in any manner, or prescribe any requirements with respect to, the administration, the personnel, the curriculum, the instruction, the methods of instruction, or the materials of instruction.

There can be no question as to the fundamental importance of such a declaration in federal aid legislation and I trust it may be possible to preserve this rock of educational liberty.

I call your attention to the fact, however, that already on the federal statute books one finds the following specifications relative to the administration of vocational education in the Smith-Hughes Act of 1917:

> . . . that such schools or classes giving instruction to persons who have not entered upon employment shall require that at least half of the time of such instruction be given to practical work on a useful or productive basis, such instruction to extend over not less than nine months per year and not less than thirty hours per week; that at least one-third of the sum appropriated to any State for the salaries of teachers of trade, home economics, and industrial subjects shall, if expended, be applied to part-time schools or classes for workers over fourteen years of age who have entered upon employment, and such subjects in a part-time school or class may mean any subject

given to enlarge the civic or vocational intelligence of such workers over fourteen and less than eighteen years of age; that such part-time schools or classes shall provide for not less than one hundred and forty-four hours of classroom instruction per year; that evening industrial schools shall fix the age of sixteen years as a minimum entrance requirement and shall confine instruction to that which is supplemental to the daily employment; that the teachers of any trade or industrial subject in any state shall have at least the minimum qualifications for teachers of such subject determined upon for such State by the State board, with the approval of the Federal Board for Vocational Education. . . . (39 Stat. 934.)

I am sure that you will agree that these prescriptions go a long way toward controlling the internal administration of the vocational education program. They should, as recommended by the President's Advisory Committee on Education in 1938, have been repealed, but as I have pointed out before, once a provision providing for federal control of education gets into a federal aid statute it seldom if ever is repealed, no matter how undesirable it may be.

Another form of federal control which has become rather usual in legislation providing federal aid to education is the requirement of state plans which must be approved by the federal agency. It is of course natural and proper that the federal agency should regularly audit the accounts of state officials in order to ascertain whether the federal funds were actually expended for the purposes specified in the legislation. It is even appropriate for the federal officials to be concerned as to the most effective means of expending the federal funds. Personally I should not object to a requirement that the respective states prepare plans which they expect to follow in the expenditure of federal funds. What seems to me entirely contrary to the spirit of state and local control in education, however, is that the federal agency should have power to accept or reject these plans. The dissemination of information including the provisions of the state plans to the court of public opinion and research studies for the profession are all that is needed in this realm. Hence there should be regularly the compilation and publication of statistical reports, supplemented by studies of special phases of the program as may be most helpful and revealing to the educational officials of the several states and to the people as a whole. State and local educational officials can and should, in the light of this information and with appropriate advice from the federal agency, make such changes in their respective state plans as seem to befit the situation in their respective states. Federal authority over state plans in education is neither necessary nor desirable.

Finally may I call your attention to the fact that in the rehabilitation act for veterans, passed two years ago, there appears the following provision: "The administrator [of the Veterans Administration] shall have the power and duty to prescribe and provide suitable training to persons . . . who are honorably discharged for disabilities connected with military service in the present war."

There we have the climax of federal control in education, or rather in training, because under the provisions of the Veterans Rehabilitation Act disabled veterans are eligible for job "training" but not for general "education." You may be interested to recall that exactly the same extensive federal control was included in the general veterans bill when it was first introduced in 1944 and was only removed after a storm of protest from the educators. One cannot be too sure, therefore, that even the so-called internal controls of education are safe indefinitely from federal invasion.

The U. S. Office of Education

To administer the responsibilities which the federal government should undertake in the field of education is a very important aspect of the subject under discussion. For the first one-half of our national existence these activities were so haphazard in character that notwithstanding the basic importance to the life of the nation attached to education by our national leaders, it did not seem necessary to set up a national office of education. When at last action to this end was taken in 1867 it was clear both from the debate in Congress at the time and from the language of the act itself that there was no intention to create a federal agency with any control over education. The new department of education (called the U. S. Office of Education since 1929) was established

for the purpose of (1) collecting such statistics and facts as shall show the condition and progress of education in the several states and territories and of (2) diffusing such information respecting the organization and management of schools and school systems and methods of teaching, as shall aid the people of the United States in the establishment and maintenance of efficient school systems, and (3) otherwise promote the cause of education throughout the country.

I am sure that you will agree that this conception of a federal office of education is entirely in harmony with the sentiments of the founding fathers with respect to the control of education. The federal agency was established as a service and promotion agency and throughout its early history it existed for this purpose alone.

There has never been a time in the history of the U. S. Office of Education when the appropriations and personnel of the Office were at all adequate to carry on its responsibilities. Henry Barnard and John Eaton, the first and second Commissioners of Education, had no professional associates — only three clerks who helped to gather and compile the statistics. Since that time, although additions have been made to the staff in the course of the years, and some extraordinarily fine services have been performed, the staff is scarcely any more adequate to its task today under present conditions than it was half a century ago.

It must be, therefore, with keen satisfaction that one examines the recent annual report of the U. S. Commissioner of Education, in which is set forth at some length the details of a proposed reorganized U. S. Office of Education along the sound lines laid down in the original legislation. At the conclusion of the proposal the Commissioner declares,

It is a legitimate function of the national service agency to influence educational programs and practices by the diffusion of trustworthy information and the exerclse of capable leadership reflecting "the organization and management of schools and school systems and methods of teaching." The exercise of influence is itself to be exclusively educational in character; hortatory and advisory rather than monitory; stimulative rather than repressive; certainly never coercive.

Here for the first time is a detailed blueprint of services which ought to be performed by a federal office of education. While one may perhaps question certain details in the plan, the proposal should receive the enthusiastic support of educators and laymen alike, in order that at long last we may have a federal agency in education fully able to perform its responsibilities effectively.

In the meantime educational activities have grown up rapidly in connection with the work of almost every federal department or major agency in Washington.

The War and Navy Departments must, of course, have their service academies, West Point, Annapolis, and New London. The activities of the Office of Indian Affairs are to a large degree educational. The Department of Agriculture is proud of its program of extension education in agriculture and home economics. The Treasury Department has its thrift educational program. The State Department is helping to support American schools, cultural centers, and libraries in Latin America. The Office of Inter-American Affairs has a whole bevy of joint agreements with Latin American countries involving the expenditure of $5,000,000. The P.W.A. supplied the funds for public school and college buildings, as well as other public buildings, and will doubtless do so again should such a program be re-established. The Department of Agriculture has a program of school lunches for children in both public and private schools. Many of the federal agencies carry on in-service programs of education for their own personnel and others.

And so it goes throughout the federal government. Few people have any idea of the variety and extent of its educational programs. One's first reaction in reviewing a list of these activities is to assume that all or practically all of them can be and should be picked up bag and baggage and handed over to the U. S. Office of Education for administration, thus presumably bringing some order out of the educational chaos in Washington. This is a rather thoughtless assumption which I have heard advanced seriously by many persons, including some educators who have not examined the problem sufficiently to appreciate its nature. To some extent it was behind the demand for a federal department of education some years ago.

Many of the educational activities carried on by

federal agencies are inherent in their primary responsibilities and cannot be separated administratively from the remaining responsibilities without reducing the program involved to ineffective dual administration. The Office of Indian Affairs is a good example. Suppose, for example, that the administration of the education of the Indians should be removed from this Office and handed over to the Office of Education. I use this example in part because such an action was seriously contemplated some years ago. After a careful examination of the subject it was decided that the education of the Indians was so intertwined with all other phases of administering the affairs of the Indians as to make it quite impossible and undesirable to divide the administrative responsibility between two different federal agencies. As a matter of fact, the education of the natives of Alaska was for a number of years carried on by the Office of Education, but there, too, the logic of the situation ultimately dictated that these educational responsibilities should be handed over to the agency which dealt with all other Alaskan affairs, namely, the Division of Territories and Island Possessions of the Interior Department. I am sure that no one would contend that it ought to be handed back to the Office of Education.

Does it follow from what I have said that no administrative duties relating to education should be assigned to the Office of Education? If so, on the basis of what principle should such assignment be made? To answer this question it may be well to remind ourselves of the original legislation creating the Office of Education, which you will recall contemplated only service and promotion activities. For many years it was felt that the addition of any kind of administrative duties, as, for example, the administration of education

for the natives of Alaska, added little if any strength
to the organization, and if multiplied several times
might indeed detract attention from the primary responsibility of the Office. It seems to me that this is
a point which, in the light of experience, deserves
serious consideration. On this subject the National
Advisory Committee on Education in its report to
President Hoover in 1931 had this interesting observa-
tion to make:

> Government bureaus that are highly endowed with political
> power, tend to resort to investigation, dissemination, and free
> argument less and less as their legal authority grows more and
> more. They tend to promote the specialty in which they are
> interested by appeals to political devices such as temptation of
> money grants, given or withheld, legal authority, and power to
> approve programs or reject them. (Page 35.)

If this policy should be adopted in the case of the
U. S. Office of Education it would mean, of course, that
the Office would confine itself to research work in
somewhat the same way as the Bureau of Standards
in the Department of Commerce; to service activities
and to general promotion. This responsibility is of
such deep moment to the most effective development
of education as a whole as to make it alone an outstanding contribution to American life. In other words,
if the full significance of some such reorganization as
is contained in the recent report of the U. S. Commissioner of Education can be realized through adequate
Congressional appropriations, it will afford the Office
of Education an opportunity for service and leadership
which would be little enhanced by additional administrative responsibilities.

I regret that I cannot take this position for the
simple reason that good administration seems to me to
make necessary, or at least desirable, that those edu-

cising any control over education in the states and localities except that which is required to implement the provisions of the United States Constitution, including the equitable distribution of federal funds for the support of white and Negro schools respectively in those states where separate schools are maintained for the two races.

9. The U. S. Office of Education should be reorganized and expanded to carry on more effectively the compilation of educational statistics, research studies in all phases of the educational program, the dissemination of information to the states and to the people on educational affairs, and the general promotion of education. To these duties should be added the administration of such acts as provide federal moneys to the states to be expended in and through schools and colleges for educational purposes.

10. There should be set up in Washington an interdepartmental council on education, which would undertake to correlate the work of the various divisions of government in the field of education. The U. S. Commissioner of Education should be the chairman of this council.